Art and Craft Skills

Printing

by Susan Niner Janes

W
FRANKLIN WATTS
Schools Library and Information Services

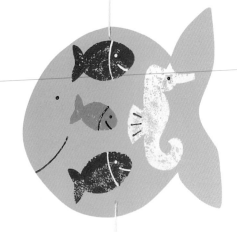

This edition 2004

First published in 1997 by
Franklin Watts,
96 Leonard Street,
London EC2A 4XD

Franklin Watts Australia,
45-51 Huntley Street,
Alexandria, NSW 2015

Copyright © Franklin Watts 1997

Series editor: Kyla Barber
Designer: Lisa Nutt
Illustrator: Lynda Murray
Photographer: Steve Shott
Art director: Robert Walster

A CIP catalogue record for this book
is available from the British Library

ISBN 0 7496 5893 2

Dewey Decimal Classification 760

Printed in Belgium

Contents

Getting started

When you print you transfer colour from one surface to another to create a pattern. Before you start, you need "the three Ps"... **p**rinters (objects to print with), **p**aper to print on (or sometimes fabric or other materials) and **p**aint (or ink). You can decorate almost anything using the printing techniques described in this book.

Basic printing methods

1 Relief printing is when a raised surface is used to print, as in stamping or potato printing.

2 Stencilling is done by dabbing paint through a cut-out shape in a piece of plastic or card.

3 Screen printing is a way to stencil more complicated designs by sticking a stencil on to mesh, or net, which is stretched across a frame.

4 Engraving is when you carve into or dent the printer to create a design. You can engrave a polystyrene food tray. The carved parts show as white.

PRINTER'S TIPS

Think before you ink! Follow these tips for successful printing sessions:

★ Thick paint prints best – runny paint makes a mess.

★ Always take a test print – and correct any faults before the real print run.

★ To print an all-over pattern, measure out placement guidelines on your paper. Mark the lines (usually as boxes – a box grid) in pencil and erase them when the paint is dry.

★ Paper colour affects paint colour. It is usually best to print on a light-coloured background. Test print first to check.

★ Always protect your work area with old newspaper. Sometimes this includes the floor as well as the table top.

★ Recycle it. Printing presents the perfect chance to recycle everyday materials such as cardboard boxes and packing materials – to print on or with.

Trace and transfer

Three steps to transfer a design:

1 Copy your design on to tracing paper.

2 Flip the design over and go over the outlines in pencil.

Practise your transferring skills on this terrapin – find out how to decorate it on page 23.

3 Turn the design back on to the right side and draw over the pencil outlines once again, or rub the design down with the back of a spoon.

Printing supplies

The basic items listed below include everything you will need to make prints. The shop key shows you where to get them.

Shop key

Art supply shop

Chemist

Supermarket

Craft or DIY shop

Stationer's

Toy shop

Art box basics

1 Greaseproof paper for low-cost tracing paper (🛒).

2 Metal ruler for measuring and cutting straight edges (🎨).

3 Scissors – use blunt-ended scissors for safety, and small pointy ones for cutting stencils (✂ 🖊 🎨).

4 Craft knife – sometimes only a very sharp blade will do. Ask an adult to do the work (🎨).

5 Masking tape prevents your work from slipping as you print it (🎨).

6 PVA glue is the best all-round glue, with a strong bond (🎨 🧸).

7 Rub-on stick glue for paper and card (🎨 ✉).

8 Black permanent-ink marker (fine-point) won't run when it gets wet (🎨 🛒).

Paper and card

9 White and coloured paper and card. Use different weights for different purposes (🎨 🧸).

10 Scrap card for cutting on or using as printing board. Use boxes from (🛒).

11 Corrugated card for printing texture or making stamps. Find it as packing material. Or buy it (🎨 🧸).

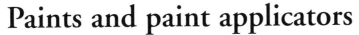

Paints and paint applicators

12 Acrylics are suitable for many surfaces including plastic and fabric. Read the label to check washability of fabric (🎨✂️).

13 Poster colours are cheap and easy to find. Ready-mixed are best (🎨🎭).

14 Fabric paints are expensive, but you may have to use these if you want to machine wash the material once you have printed (🎨✂️).

15 Paintbrushes – use small ones for painting your designs, wide ones for backgrounds (🎨🎭).

16 Sponge rollers and brushes are useful for colouring large areas quickly (🎨🎭).

17 Sponges – for stencilling and making textures. Different types produce different effects (🛒🔪).

Tricks of the trade

18 Clear plastic folders or looseleaf pockets make cheap stencil and printing material, or paint palettes. Can be used as an alternative to acetate sheet, below. Cut the pocket into two separate sheets to use it (✉️).

19 Acetate sheet can be used for monoprinting and comb-transfer printing. Wash it after printing so you can use it more than once (✉️).

20 Craft foam is useful for making stamps (🎨✂️).

21 Polystyrene food trays make good printing plates, and disposable palettes (🛒).

22 Thick felt-tip pens – use for inking stamps (✉️🎨🎭).

23 Decorative edging scissors (pinking shears) are good for tidying edges (🎨🎭✂️).

Keep it Tidy!

Make sure you have these things to hand before you start –

- ◎ An old T-shirt or adult-sized shirt – instant artist's smock.
- ◎ Old newspapers for protecting work surfaces.
- ◎ Clean rags, old towels or kitchen roll.
- ◎ Washing-up liquid.

7

Stamping

Stamps are good for producing repeating patterns. They are easy to make from craft foam, card or kitchen sponge. Remember to keep the designs simple. Try the bird shapes below.

You will need

- ★ craft foam
- ★ thick felt-tip pens
- ★ coloured paper and card
- ★ permanent marker pen
- ★ rub-on glue stick
- ★ cardboard
- ★ PVA glue
- ★ scissors
- ★ masking tape
- ★ pencil ★ ruler

Additional Materials: ★ coloured envelopes

1 Sketch your designs on paper – keep them simple – you can draw details on to the print later. Also, remember the design will print back to front.

2 Transfer or copy the design on to craft foam. Cut it out and glue it on to cardboard. If you want to use two colours, mark out the dividing line with a pen.

3 Colour in the raised part of the stamp with thick felt-tip pens. Tape your printing paper to a surface. Press the stamp firmly on to it.

4 Lift the stamp off gently. You can complete the stamp print by drawing in the details (like the eyes and legs of the bird).

Notecard holder

Cut out a birdhouse shape from cardboard. Cut an envelope in half and stamp designs on it. Then glue it to the card and use it to store stamped notecards. Attach a card loop to hold a pencil.

Now try these

A Rainy Day
Stamps can be used to make simple clouds, umbrellas and raindrops. Pick a theme and see how many stamps you can make to create a picture.

Notepaper
To make personalised notepaper, stamp patterns along the edge of the paper.

Flowers and Leaves
Use kitchen sponge to make simple flower shaped stamps – colour the petals a different shade to the centre.

Making tracks

You have "instant printers" attached to your body – your hands and feet. Using them can be messy, so wear old clothes and keep a bucket of warm soapy water nearby. You can make your prints into boats, faces, animals or even monsters by adding just a few details.

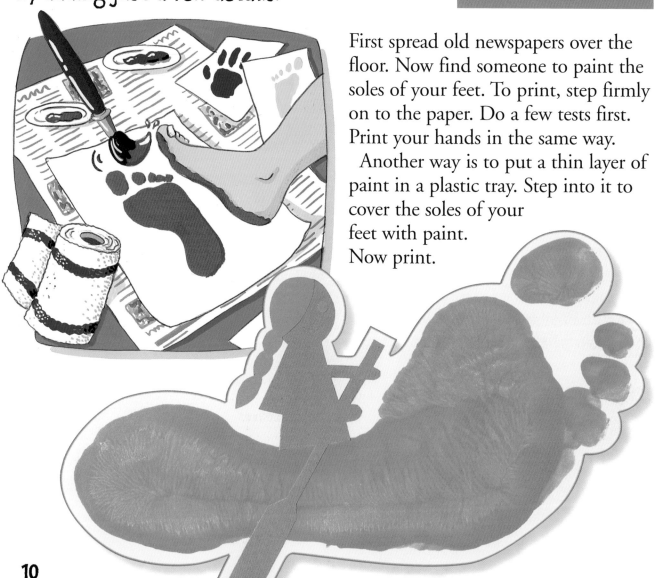

First spread old newspapers over the floor. Now find someone to paint the soles of your feet. To print, step firmly on to the paper. Do a few tests first. Print your hands in the same way.

Another way is to put a thin layer of paint in a plastic tray. Step into it to cover the soles of your feet with paint. Now print.

Adding details

Making hand and footprint pictures is a bit like looking at clouds . . . there's no telling what your imagination will see. Add glued-on paper eyes, mouths, glasses, antennae or clothes to make your prints come alive.

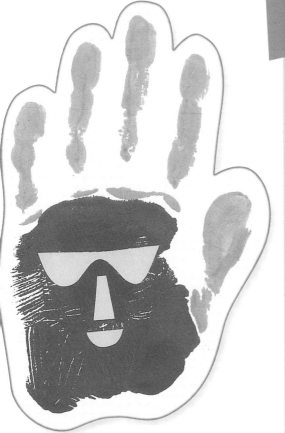

Now try these

Alien Mobile
Print foot and hand prints and decorate them with glued-on paper shapes. Make a small hole in the top of each print and tie on thread. Attach the threads to a wire hanger to make a mobile.

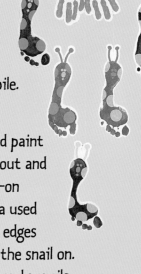

Snail Tin
Print a footprint and paint on antennae. Cut it out and decorate with glued-on paper shapes. Paint a used tin (cover any sharp edges with tape) and glue the snail on. Use it to store pens and pencils.

Anything prints

If you can brush an object with paint, you can probably print with it. To make these puppets, print patterns using ordinary and easily found things.

The basics

Remember to ask an adult's permission before printing with anything you find.

For many objects, all you have to do is brush on paint and stamp it on to the paper. Use thick and creamy paint.

To make small objects easier to handle, stick them on to backing card with glue or poster putty.

To make an evenly spaced repeating pattern, you may want to measure out a pencil grid.

To print large surfaces, use bubble wrap or corrugated card.

Always wash and dry the printers after use.

Jumbo stick puppets

Make lots of bold prints on paper. Now cut simple puppet shapes from card. Cut out and glue your prints on to the shapes. Add faces. Tightly roll up a sheet of thick paper to make a handle.

Printers used here:

Princess's coat: satsuma peel stuck on to card.

Jester's mask: toy car tyre and an eraser.

The big, bold patterns were printed with the ends of foam building bricks.

Now try these

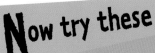

Jester's Mask
Print and cut out a mask and a hat then glue them together. Glue paper "bells" on to the hat points.

Snail Spinner
Cut a snail shape and stick it on to card. Wind a piece of thick string or wool on to backing card to make a stamp. Decorate the snail. Make a snail spinning top.

PRINTER'S TIP
◎ Poster paints may "bead up" on plastic. To make the paint stick, add a little washing-up liquid.

Sponge stencilling

Cut a shape into card or plastic then sponge paint into the cut-out space. This is stencilling. The sponge creates a bubbly texture, just right for a fishy scene.

You will need

- ★ clear plastic pockets
- ★ black permanent marker
- ★ acrylic or poster paints
- ★ masking tape
- ★ squeezy fabric paint
- ★ kitchen sponge cloths
- ★ small scissors
- ★ a sponge
- ★ mixing brush
- ★ coloured card
- ★ string

1 Draw your design on a piece of paper. Cut a piece of plastic and slip the paper under it. Trace the design on to the plastic with a permanent marker.

2 Make a snip in the centre of the plastic, then cut to reach the outline. Snip around the outline, then remove the centre. Make other undersea stencils.

3 Tape the stencil in place. The see-through plastic makes it easy to position. Pour a little thick and creamy paint on to your palette. You may have to thin the paint with a drop or two of water. Use a mixing brush.

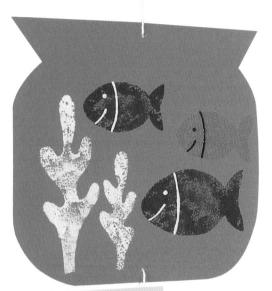

4 Cut some sponge and dip the end in the paint. Blot it on the palette, then dab paint on to the stencil opening. Start at the edges of the stencil, taking care at corners, then do the centre.

Fishy mobile

Cut large undersea shapes from coloured card. Using your stencils, decorate each shape and add details with squeezy fabric paint. Pierce holes in the card shapes and join them with string.

PRINTER'S TIPS

★ Always remember to wipe your stencil before printing the next shape.
★ Try different sponges for different effects.

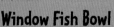

Fishy Cards

Draw a fish shape on to folded card. Cut the fish out – take care not to cut the fold. Stencil on decoration.

Window Fish Bowl

Cut a fish bowl hole in card. Stencil fish on to a piece of clear plastic with acrylic paints. Tape it behind the fish bowl and hang it in the window.

Potato prints

Potato printing is a quick and easy way to make clean, sharp prints. It is a kind of "relief" printing, which means printing with a raised surface. Carve different shapes and experiment with colours, patterns or pictures.

You will need

- ◆ a craft knife ◆ acrylic paints or poster colours ◆ flat brush
- ◆ cartridge paper ◆ scissors ◆ paper ◆ card ◆ PVA glue

Additional Materials:
- ◆ large, clean potatoes ◆ kitchen knife ◆ straight pins

1 Protect your work area with old newspaper. Cut the potato in half lengthwise. The cut surface must be flat and smooth.

ASK AN ADULT FOR HELP

2 Design a pattern to fit on the potato surface and cut out a paper template. Fix in place with straight pins. Cut away the potato where you don't want it to print. Remove the template.

3 Blot the printing surface with kitchen paper to remove any juice (potato juice thins the paint and makes it slippery). Brush on the paint.

4 To print, press the potato block firmly, straight on to the paper. Then "lift off" quickly and cleanly. You may be able to make a second print from one inking.

Magic party hat

Cut out a top hat shape in black card. Decorate a paper strip with potato prints and stick it to the hat.

Glue a 60cm-strip of card on to the back of the hat, along the bottom edge. Glue the ends of the strip together to fit your head.

Now try this

Pond Life
Print a complete picture using simple potato print shapes – fish, lily leaves and flowers are easy things to start with. Try harder shapes when you feel confident.

Magician's scarf

Take a scarf-sized piece of card, cover it in clingfilm and tape a square of material tightly on to it. Print with glue instead of paint. Sprinkle glitter over the "glue prints".

Simple engraving

Polystyrene trays used for packing supermarket food are ideal for making engraved printing blocks. To mark a picture in the soft material, simply press into it with a pointy tool. When the block is inked, the engraved outline shows as white or your paper colour.

You will need

- ★ polystyrene food trays
- ★ printing paper
- ★ a nail or sharp pencil
- ★ scrap card   ★ scissors
- ★ ballpoint pen   ★ glue stick
- ★ acrylic or poster paints
- ★ wide paintbrush

1 If the tray has sides, cut them off. Plan your design on paper, then lightly pencil it on to the tray.

2 For a dotted outline use a nail, awl or sharp pencil to prick holes along the outline. For a plain line, press firmly with a ballpoint pen.

3 Tape down the print block. Brush or sponge paint on evenly. Lay a piece of paper on top and smooth it gently. Lift the print off, then wipe the block clean.

Ship cards

Print a ship on a piece of light-coloured card. Cut around the ship and glue it on to a piece of folded card.

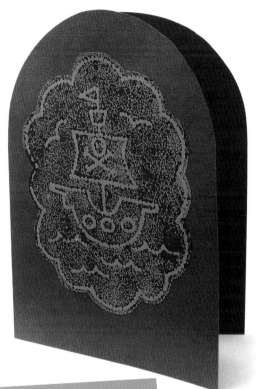

PRINTER'S TIPS

★ Try engraving your design into thick cardboard, or the back of corrugated card for a similar effect.

★ Try printing with foam ceiling tiles – they come in a variety of textures. Ask an adult to help you cut them.

Now try these

Bird

Make a bird print on stiff paper and cut it out. Cut a piece of paper and concertina fold it to make the wings. Use a pair of scissors and carefully make a slit in the centre of the bird and push the folded wings through.

Strawberry Note Pad

Draw a strawberry on to polystyrene with a thin brush dipped in nail varnish remover. The polystyrene will dissolve where you've brushed. The leaves at the top are stencilled.

ASK AN ADULT FOR HELP

Only use nail varnish remover when an adult is present

Monoprints

Draw a simple line design on paper, slip it under a sheet of clear plastic and you have created an instant printing press. Simply paint over the lines of your design and take a print. Try these simple lantern shapes first then experiment with more complicated designs.

1 Draw a simple, two-coloured design. This will be a printing guide – the monoprint will not be a perfect copy as the paint spreads as it is printed.

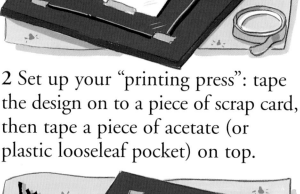

2 Set up your "printing press": tape the design on to a piece of scrap card, then tape a piece of acetate (or plastic looseleaf pocket) on top.

3 Paint the lines of your design on the acetate, then lower a piece of paper on top. Smooth the paper lightly so the paint touches – don't press too hard.

4 Lift the print off carefully, then wipe the acetate clean with a cloth. You are ready to start on the next print.

Lantern card

Print six lanterns on plain paper. Tear around each one. Thread them on to a piece of wool, then glue them on to card.

PRINTER'S TIP

◉ Poster paints may "bead up" on plastic. To make the paint stick, add a little washing-up liquid.

◉ To make complicated, multi-coloured monoprints, print each colour separately.

You must make sure that your paper is in the same position each time you print a new colour. Draw lines on the acetate that match up with the corners of your printing paper.

Now try these

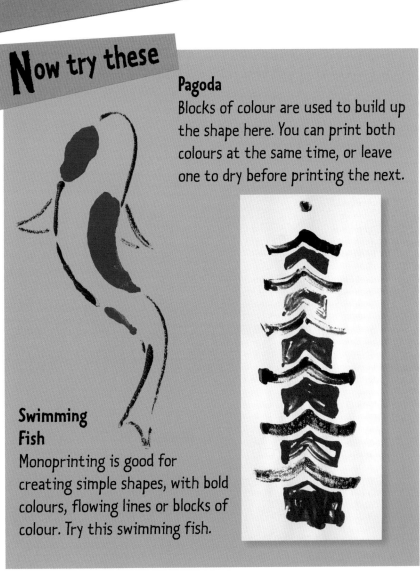

Pagoda

Blocks of colour are used to build up the shape here. You can print both colours at the same time, or leave one to dry before printing the next.

Swimming Fish

Monoprinting is good for creating simple shapes, with bold colours, flowing lines or blocks of colour. Try this swimming fish.

Corrugated quilling

These stamps, made from coiled strips of corrugated card, create lacy patterns. The rolled shapes are inspired by the papercraft called "quilling". Each stamp can be used many times.

You will need:

- corrugated card
- PVA glue
- scissors
- rub-on glue stick
- coloured card and paper
- decorative edging scissors (pinking shears)
- cardboard
- ruler
- glue spreader
- pencil

Quilling shape chart

Cut a strip of corrugated card, about 3cm by 18cm. Curl the strip to make the shape you want.

Closed shapes

Tight coil: roll the strip tightly. Glue the end.

Eye: make a loose coil. Pinch opposite sides.

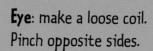

Teardrop: make a loose coil. Pinch one side.

Square: make a loose coil. Pinch to make four corners.

Loose coil: roll the strip loosely. Glue the end.

Triangle: make a loose coil. Pinch to make three corners.

Open shapes

Roller: make a V-shape and roll each end outwards

Scroll: take a strip, curl opposite ends towards centre.

Heart: pinch the scroll above to make a centre V.

Ceremonial elephant

Copy the elephant shape below on to coloured card, and cut it out. Cut out the ear and the tusk separately. Cut out a blanket in contrasting colour card. Use your corrugated stamps to print patterns. Glue on the blanket, tusk and ear.

Now try these

Mosaic Terrapin

Copy or trace a terrapin on to card and cut it out. Cut tile shapes from a different-coloured card, and stamp them with a corrugated stamp. Glue them down to create the terrapin's shell.

Jack's Vest

Print rows of pattern shapes on brightly coloured papers. Cut out the rows. Cut out a card person. Cut the rows to make up a vest shape, and glue them on the person.

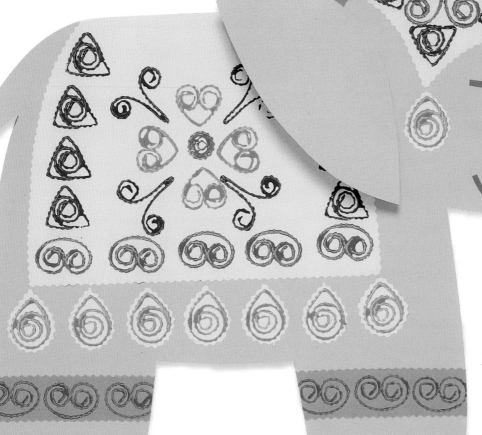

Roller printing

Rollers are perfect for printing borders or for making all-over patterns. Here are two types of rollers for you to make – pattern rollers and texture rollers.

You will need

- ★ sponge rollers
- ★ card
- ★ PVA glue
- ★ string
- ★ ruler
- ★ scissors
- ★ corrugated card
- ★ pencils

Additional Materials:
- ★ holepunch
- ★ toilet roll tubes
- ★ felt

Pattern rollers

1 Take a toilet roll tube, trace the ends on to card and cut two circles. Punch a hole in the centre of each. Glue or tape the circles on to both ends of the tube. Push a pencil through.

2 Glue a strip of card around the tube and trim it so the ends don't overlap. Draw three or four shapes on some cardboard and cut them out. Glue the card shapes on to the roller. Space them evenly.

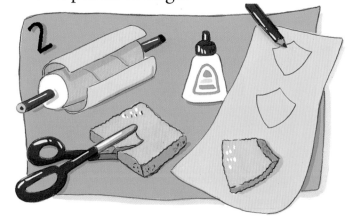

Texture rollers

Corrugated Card Roller
Make a basic roller (as before), then glue on corrugated card.

Stripy Sponge Roller
Tie a bought sponge roller with pieces of string. It will print uneven stripes.

Picture frames

Cut four strips of card. Print them in a bold colour using a corrugated card roller. Glue the strips together, as shown. Stick on backing board, leaving one side unglued so you can slip in a picture.

Now try these

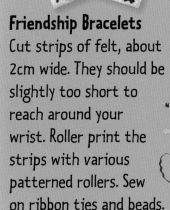

Friendship Bracelets
Cut strips of felt, about 2cm wide. They should be slightly too short to reach around your wrist. Roller print the strips with various patterned rollers. Sew on ribbon ties and beads.

More Frames
Decorate large envelopes with a textured roller, then a patterned roller. Cut out a space from the centre to make room for a picture.

PRINTER'S TIP
★ Roller prints fade as you print. You can either leave the result as it is or touch it up with paint.

Combing

Using a notched-card comb, you can scrape paint off an inked surface to create swirls and zigzags. The print is then transferred on to paper. Print patterns, pictures and even hairstyles.

You will need

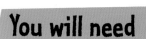

- a wide brush
- safety pins
- card
- coloured paper
- scissors
- glue stick
- clear plastic sheet
- ribbon
- masking tape
- kitchen roll or rags
- sticky tape
- acrylic or poster paint

1 Cut out mini combs from stiff card. Make combs with two, three and four teeth. You will also need a few plain card scrapers without teeth.

2 Tape an acetate or plastic sheet on to a piece of scrap card. Brush on paint evenly. Now you are ready to comb your patterns.

3 Make squiggles, zigzags or loops with the combs; straighter lines need simple strokes. For a decorative bow, twist a plain piece of card.

4 To print, smooth a piece of paper over the pattern – don't press too hard. Peel the paper off quickly. Wipe the acetate and you are ready to start again.

Badges

To make badges, snip out a hairstyle from the print and glue it on to card. Add a paper cut-out face. Cut around each badge. You can glue on a bow. Fix a safety pin to the back of the badge with a strip of sticky tape.

Now try this

Zebra
Use the combing method with black paint and white paper. Then cut out a zebra shape. You can add the mane and tail separately.

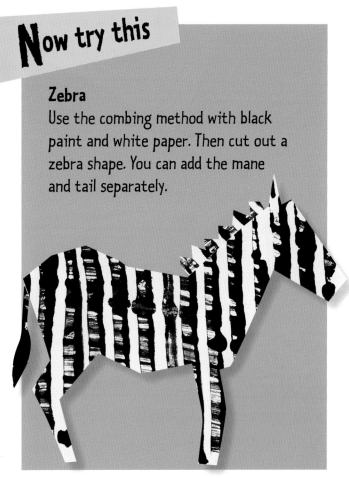

Printing blocks

A printing block is a stamp that can be made up of different materials. Try to choose a variety of objects that will produce interesting textures when they are printed. For instance, the robot below is made up from corrugated card, craft foam and cardboard.

You will need

★ cardboard ★ PVA glue ★ pencil
★ corrugated card ★ scissors
★ craft foam ★ brushes
★ masking tape ★ paper
Additional Materials:
★ silver paint ★ sticky stars
★ silver marker

1 Plan your design on paper – keep it bold and simple. Trace the design on to the backing card.

2 Cut the shapes out of as many different materials as you can find and glue them in place on the backing card.

3 Tape the printing block down. Brush paint on to its raised parts. Work quickly so the paint doesn't dry.

4 Press paper on to the printing block and smooth it down. Don't miss any of the raised printing areas. Gently lift it off.

Robot in a rocket

Print a robot and add details with silver felt-tip. Cut a rocket-shaped hole from blue card, add sticky stars around the edge. Glue the robot print behind the hole.

Now try these

Bits and Pieces
Glue wound string on to a block to make a balloon, add a basket from corrugated card and clouds from bubble wrap. Take a print.

Pasta Bugs
Stick pasta shapes on to cardboard – perfect for insect prints.

Money Spider
Make a printing block out of coins. Wash your money when you've finished.

PRINTER'S TIP
★ Use printing materials that are textured and easy to cut: polystyrene food trays, corrugated card, bubble wrap.

Screen printing

Net stencilling is an easy type of screen printing and is good for printing fabric. You can also try printing a shape-within-a-stencil as with this T-shirt design.

You will need

- card
- sponge
- ruler
- acrylic or fabric paints
- craft knife
- stapler
- net fabric
- small scissors
- masking tape
- bulldog clips
- pencil
- paper

Additional Materials:

- clear sticky backed plastic
- plain cotton T-shirt
- clingfilm

ASK AN ADULT FOR HELP

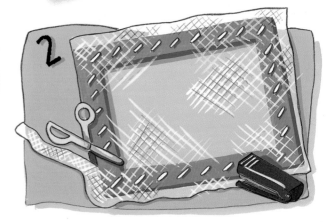

1 Plan your stencil design on paper. Ask an adult to cut out a window shape in thick card, using a craft knife and ruler. The card frame must be larger than your stencil design.

2 Cut a piece of net slightly larger all round than the frame. Staple the net on to the frame. The net should be completely tight. Trim the net around the frame.

3 Trace the design on to sticky backed plastic. Snip into the plastic and cut around line. Now snip out the centre shape (here a heart) and keep it. Peel the backing off the plastic and smooth the stencil on to the net. Stick on the centre shape too. The areas of mesh that are not covered with plastic will print.

4 Insert a piece of clingfilm-covered card to keep the T-shirt taut. Take up any slack material with bulldog clips. Tape on the stencil, then sponge on the paint. Remove the tape and carefully lift off the stencil.

"Triple-T" T-Shirt

You can make a net stencil for three different stencil designs. Print each in a different colour in a row on your T-shirt. Wait until each print is dry before going on to the next.

PRINTER'S TIP
◆ If the net clogs up, clear it with a pin.

Now try these

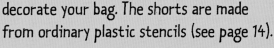

Decorate Your Gym Bag
You can use net stencilling to print on your gym bag. Use the T-shirt stencil to decorate your bag. The shorts are made from ordinary plastic stencils (see page 14).

Fire! Make a fiery net stencil and dab yellow paint through the openings on to black paper. When dry, repeat using orange then red paint. Move your stencil each time you print.

Glossary

comb printing Card combs can be used to make patterns and swirls in paint. The combed patterns create interesting prints (pages 26–27).

engraving Create a pattern by carving or pressing into a soft material, such as polystyrene, foam or thick card. When you take a print the pattern shows up as white, or the colour of your paper (pages 4, 18–19).

monoprinting This is a one-off print, made from painting a flat surface then transferring the paint on to paper. As the pattern is repainted each time, every monoprint is slightly different (pages 20–21).

potato printing A raised shape can be created by carving into a halved potato. It can then be used as a printing stamp (pages 16–17).

printing Paint is transferred from one surface to another.

printing block A pattern is made up from gluing lots of different materials on to backing card. The raised surface is painted and used for printing (pages 28–29).

roller printing A roller can make interesting prints. You can add a textured surface to the roller, or shapes cut from card, so that the roller makes a pattern as it goes (pages 24–25).

screen printing A stencil is made from either card or plastic and is stuck on to a mesh-covered frame. The mesh or net is then painted. You can use this technique to print on fabric (pages 30–31).

sponge stencilling A stencil is cut out of card or plastic. Paint is sponged on to the paper through the stencil opening (pages 14–15).

stamping Simple shapes cut from card or foam are stuck on to a piece of backing card. The raised surface is covered with paint or ink, and used to print shapes (pages 8–9, 12, 22–23).

Index